**TRANSFORM YOUR SPACE
TRANSFORM YOUR LIFE**

THE
WELLBEING
DESIGN
TOOLKIT

**TRANSFORM YOUR SPACE
TRANSFORM YOUR LIFE**

**TRANSFORM YOUR SPACE
TRANSFORM YOUR LIFE**

**Copyright ©Frven Lim, 2025
2nd Edition**

All rights reserved. No part of this publication may be reproduced, distributed, or transmitted in any form or by any means, including photocopying, recording, or other electronic or mechanical methods, without the prior written permission of the publisher, except in the case of brief quotations embodied in critical reviews and certain other noncommercial uses permitted by copyright law.

**TRANSFORM YOUR SPACE
TRANSFORM YOUR LIFE**

**TRANSFORM YOUR SPACE
TRANSFORM YOUR LIFE**

This toolkit comprises worksheets that directly reference the chapters in "Wellbeing + Happiness Thru' Architecture + Design" by Frven Lim.

The exercises will encourage high engagement and applies the concepts presented in the book. Its core purpose is to facilitate readers to interact with the material actively, making personal connections with the book content through exercises, reflections, and actionable steps.

Suggestion:
Pace it out and complete the worksheets weekly, ideally alongside the corresponding chapter of the book that you have read.

**TRANSFORM YOUR SPACE
TRANSFORM YOUR LIFE**

START
YOUR
JOURNEY

TRANSFORM YOUR SPACE
TRANSFORM YOUR LIFE

CONTENTS

Chapter 1 Worksheets: ... 9
Small but Big aka #SBB
Worksheet 1.1: Identifying SBB Changes
Worksheet 1.2: Action Plan for SBB Changes

Chapter 2 Worksheets: ... 16
The EUREKA of WHAD
Worksheet 2.1: Eureka Moments Log
Worksheet 2.2: Design Your Eureka Project

Chapter 3 Worksheets: ... 23
Curiosity and Competence
Worksheet 3.1: Curiosity Inventory
Worksheet 3.2: Competence Building Plan

Chapter 4 Worksheets: ... 30
Six Senses
Worksheet 4.1: Sensory Exploration Log
Worksheet 4.2: Sensory Design Challenge

Chapter 5 Worksheets: ... 37
The Power of Materiality
Worksheet 5.1: Material Mood Board
Worksheet 5.2: Material Experimentation

**TRANSFORM YOUR SPACE
TRANSFORM YOUR LIFE**

Chapter 6 Worksheets: ... 45
Understanding the Functions of Spaces
Worksheet 6.1: Space Function Analysis
Worksheet 6.2: Space Redesign Plan

Chapter 7 Worksheets: ... 52
Modern Day Cavemen
Worksheet 7.1: Primal Needs Assessment
Worksheet 7.2: Enhancing Primal Comforts

Chapter 8 Worksheets: ... 59
Tribes
Worksheet 8.1: Social Space Audit
Worksheet 8.2: Designing for Community

Chapter 9 Worksheets: ... 67
DKZzzz (Dining/Kitchen/Sleep)
Worksheet 9.1: DKZzz Analysis
Worksheet 9.2: Wellbeing Enhancement Plan

Chapter 10 Worksheets: ... 76
How to WHAD Ahead?
Worksheet 10.1: WHAD Reflection
Worksheet 10.2: WHAD Action Plan

TRANSFORM YOUR SPACE
TRANSFORM YOUR LIFE

LET'S START!

**TRANSFORM YOUR SPACE
TRANSFORM YOUR LIFE**

These worksheets aim to guide the reader through a process of recognising small changes that can significantly impact their wellbeing and happiness through architecture and design.

Chapter 1 Worksheets:

Small but Big aka #SBB

Worksheet 1.1: Identifying Small But Big Changes

Objective:
To help readers identify small, achievable changes in their environments that align with the WHAD principles for enhancing wellbeing and happiness.

TRANSFORM YOUR SPACE
TRANSFORM YOUR LIFE

Instructions:
Reflect on Your Space: Take a moment to think about your personal and workspaces. How do you feel in these spaces? List down immediate feelings or thoughts that come to mind.

Identify Small Changes:

Consider small aspects of your environment that could be altered to improve your wellbeing.
Use the following prompts to guide your thinking:

- **Lighting:** Could changing the lighting (e.g., brighter bulbs, softer lights, more natural light) alter the mood of your space?

- **Colour**: Are there colours that make you feel more relaxed or energised? Consider how adding these colours through paint, decorations, or textiles could impact your space.

- **Nature**: How could you incorporate elements of nature (e.g., plants, water features, natural materials) into your environment?

- **Organisation**: Would decluttering or reorganising your space make it more functional and serene?

- **Personal Touches**: Are there any personal items, photos, or artwork that could make your space feel more "you"?

TRANSFORM YOUR SPACE
TRANSFORM YOUR LIFE

Worksheet:

- **Space**: (e.g., home office, bedroom, living area)

- **Current Feelings/Thoughts**:

TRANSFORM YOUR SPACE
TRANSFORM YOUR LIFE

- **Identified Changes**:

    - Lighting:

    - Colour:

    - Nature:

    - Organisation:

    - Personal Touches:

- **Expected Outcome**: How do you think these changes will impact your wellbeing and happiness?

**TRANSFORM YOUR SPACE
TRANSFORM YOUR LIFE**

Worksheet 1.2: Action Plan for Small But Big Changes

Objective:
To create a detailed plan for implementing the small changes identified in Worksheet 1.1, encouraging readers to take action towards enhancing their environment.

Instructions:

- **Prioritise Changes**: Based on Worksheet 1.1, choose the top three changes you're most excited about and believe will have the most significant impact.

- **Detail Your Action Steps**: For each change, outline specific steps needed to implement this change. Include resources required, such as materials, tools, or help from others.

- **Set Deadlines**: Assign a realistic deadline for completing each change. Consider your current commitments and pace yourself to avoid overwhelm.

- **Visualise Success**: For each change, describe how the successful implementation will alter your space and its effect on your wellbeing.

**TRANSFORM YOUR SPACE
TRANSFORM YOUR LIFE**

Worksheet:

- Change 1:
    - Action Steps:
    - Resources Needed:
    - Deadline:
    - Visualised Outcome:

- Change 2:
    - Action Steps:
    - Resources Needed:
    - Deadline:
    - Visualised Outcome:

**TRANSFORM YOUR SPACE
TRANSFORM YOUR LIFE**

- **Change 3:**

  - **Action Steps:**

  - **Resources Needed:**

  - **Deadline:**

  - **Visualised Outcome:**

These worksheets are designed to guide readers through a reflective and actionable process, moving from recognising small but significant enhancements to actively planning and implementing changes that foster wellbeing and happiness through their environment.

**TRANSFORM YOUR SPACE
TRANSFORM YOUR LIFE**

These exercises are aimed at encouraging readers to see their spaces in new lights and to conceptualise projects that embody the chapter's principles.

Chapter 2 Worksheets:

The EUREKA of WHAD

Worksheet 2.1: Eureka Moments Log

Objective:
To help readers record and reflect on past eureka moments related to their environment, facilitating a deeper understanding of how spaces can significantly influence their state of wellbeing.

TRANSFORM YOUR SPACE
TRANSFORM YOUR LIFE

Instructions:

- **Recall and Record Eureka Moments**: Think back to any moments when a change or realisation about your physical environment significantly impacted your mood, productivity, or wellbeing. Describe each moment, focusing on what changed or what realisation occurred.

- **Analyse the Impact**: For each moment listed, analyze how the change or realisation affected you. Did it lead to improved productivity, mood enhancement, or a greater sense of happiness?

- **Draw Insights**: Reflect on the common themes or elements from your eureka moments. Are there specific types of changes (e.g., lighting, space organisation, addition of plants) that consistently lead to positive outcomes for you?

TRANSFORM YOUR SPACE
TRANSFORM YOUR LIFE

Worksheet:

- **Eureka Moment 1:**

    - **Description:**
    - **Impact:**
    - **Insights:**

- **Eureka Moment 2:**

    - **Description:**
    - **Impact:**
    - **Insights:**

TRANSFORM YOUR SPACE
TRANSFORM YOUR LIFE

(Continue as needed)

**TRANSFORM YOUR SPACE
TRANSFORM YOUR LIFE**

Worksheet 2.2: Design Your Eureka Project

Objective:
To guide readers in conceptualising a design project for their personal or work space that integrates the insights from their eureka moments, with the aim of enhancing wellbeing and happiness.

Instructions:

- **Define Your Project**: Based on the insights from Worksheet 2.1, define a project that aims to recreate or introduce a 'eureka' effect in your chosen space. Describe the space and the intended outcome.

- **Outline Design Elements**: Identify the design elements (e.g., colour schemes, materials, lighting, spatial arrangements) that will be central to achieving the intended outcome. Reference specific insights or moments from Worksheet 2.1 where applicable.

- **Plan the Implementation**: Break down the project into manageable steps, including any research, purchases, or help you'll need. Set a realistic timeline for each step.

- **Visualise the Outcome**: Describe how the successful completion of this project will transform the space and its anticipated impact on your wellbeing.

**TRANSFORM YOUR SPACE
TRANSFORM YOUR LIFE**

Worksheet:

- **Project Description**:
- **Space Targeted**:
- **Intended Outcome**:

  - **Design Elements**:
  - Colour Schemes:
  - Materials:
  - Lighting:
  - Spatial Arrangements:
  - **Implementation Plan**:
  - Step 1:
  - Step 2:
- **Timeline**:

**TRANSFORM YOUR SPACE
TRANSFORM YOUR LIFE**

- **Visualised Outcome:**

 These worksheets are crafted to facilitate a practical application of Chapter 2's core message, encouraging readers to intentionally engage with their environments to unlock the full potential of their spaces in enhancing wellbeing and happiness.

**TRANSFORM YOUR SPACE
TRANSFORM YOUR LIFE**

The following detailed worksheets are designed to inspire readers to embrace a mindset of continuous learning and humility. This chapter encourages exploring unknowns within the realm of architecture and design as a path to enhancing wellbeing and happiness.

Chapter 3 Worksheets:

Curiosity and Competence

Worksheet 3.1: Curiosity Inventory

Objective:
To assess the reader's level of curiosity about their surroundings and their willingness to learn new things about architecture, design, and their impact on wellbeing.

TRANSFORM YOUR SPACE
TRANSFORM YOUR LIFE

Instructions:

- **Rate Your Curiosity**: On a scale of 1 to 10, rate your current level of curiosity about how architectural and design elements affect wellbeing.

- **Identify Areas of Interest**: List areas within architecture and design you're most curious about (e.g., sustainable materials, ergonomic design, space utilisation).

- **Knowledge Gaps**: For each area of interest, note down what you know already and what you'd like to learn more about.

- **Action Steps**: Based on your knowledge gaps, outline steps you could take to learn more (e.g., books to read, courses to take, places to visit).

**TRANSFORM YOUR SPACE
TRANSFORM YOUR LIFE**

Worksheet:

- **Curiosity Level**
- **Areas of Interest**:
    - Area 1:
    - What I Know:
    - What I Want to Learn:
    - Action Steps:

    - Area 2:
    - What I Know:
    - What I Want to Learn:
    - Action Steps:

**TRANSFORM YOUR SPACE
TRANSFORM YOUR LIFE**

(Continue as needed)

TRANSFORM YOUR SPACE
TRANSFORM YOUR LIFE

Worksheet 3.2: Competence Building Plan

Objective: To create a structured plan for readers to improve or acquire new skills and knowledge in areas of architecture and design they are curious about, to enhance personal and environmental wellbeing.

Instructions:

- **Set Learning Goals**: Based on the areas of interest identified in Worksheet 3.1, set specific learning goals for each area.

- **Resources and Methods**: For each learning goal, identify resources (books, online courses, workshops) and methods (self-study, mentorship, practical projects) to achieve these goals.

- **Timeline**: Assign a realistic timeline to each learning goal, taking into account your current commitments and learning pace.

- **Reflection and Application**: Plan how you will apply the new knowledge or skills to your environment. Consider small projects or changes you can implement as you learn.

**TRANSFORM YOUR SPACE
TRANSFORM YOUR LIFE**

Worksheet:

- **Learning Goal 1:**
    - **Resources & Methods:**
    - **Timeline:**
    - **Application:**

- **Learning Goal 2:**
    - **Resources & Methods:**
    - **Timeline:**
    - **Application:**

**TRANSFORM YOUR SPACE
TRANSFORM YOUR LIFE**

(Continue as needed)

These worksheets aim to guide readers through recognising their curiosity and knowledge gaps, setting actionable learning goals, and applying new knowledge to enhance their environmental wellbeing. The emphasis is on the value of continuous learning and the positive impact of this growth mindset on personal wellbeing and the quality of designed spaces.

**TRANSFORM YOUR SPACE
TRANSFORM YOUR LIFE**

The following detailed worksheets are designed to engage readers in exploring how their sensory experiences are influenced by their environment. This chapter delves into the profound impact that nurturing all six senses (including intuition beyond the traditional five) can have on wellbeing and happiness in spaces designed with architectural and design principles in mind.

Chapter 4 Worksheets: Six Senses

Worksheet 4.1: Sensory Exploration Log

Objective:
To guide readers through a reflective exploration of how each of their senses currently interacts with their personal and work environments, highlighting areas for enhancement.

TRANSFORM YOUR SPACE
TRANSFORM YOUR LIFE

Instructions:

- **Document Sensory Experiences**: Over the next week, take note of how each sense is stimulated in your key environments. Record both positive and negative experiences.

- **Assessment**: After a week, assess your log. Identify patterns or specific elements that consistently contribute to your wellbeing or discomfort.

- **Enhancement Ideas**: Based on your assessment, brainstorm ideas on how you could enhance each sensory experience in your environment.

**TRANSFORM YOUR SPACE
TRANSFORM YOUR LIFE**

Worksheet:

- **Sense**: Sight
    - **Positive Experiences**:
    - **Negative Experiences**:
    - **Enhancement Ideas**:

- **Sense**: Hearing
    - **Positive Experiences**:
    - **Negative Experiences**:
    - **Enhancement Ideas**:

**TRANSFORM YOUR SPACE
TRANSFORM YOUR LIFE**

(Continue with Smell, Taste, Touch, and Intuition)

TRANSFORM YOUR SPACE
TRANSFORM YOUR LIFE

Worksheet 4.2: Sensory Design Challenge

Objective: Encourages readers to redesign a small aspect of their environment with a focus on improving sensory experiences, utilising insights from their exploration log.

Instructions:

- **Choose a Focus Area**: Select one sense you wish to enhance in a specific part of your environment (e.g., sight in the living room).

- **Design Concept**: Develop a design concept that addresses the sensory enhancement. Consider colours, materials, lighting, soundproofing, scent diffusion, etc.

- **Implementation Plan**: Outline the steps needed to bring your design concept to life, including any materials, tools, or assistance required.

- **Expected Impact**: Describe how this enhancement will change the sensory experience and its anticipated effect on your overall wellbeing.

**TRANSFORM YOUR SPACE
TRANSFORM YOUR LIFE**

Worksheet:

- **Focus Sense & Area:**
  - **Design Concept:**
  - **Elements to Introduce or Modify:**

  - **Implementation Plan:**
  - Step 1:

  - Step 2:

  - (Continue as needed)

**TRANSFORM YOUR SPACE
TRANSFORM YOUR LIFE**

- **Timeline:**

- **Expected Impact on Wellbeing:**

These worksheets are intended to make readers more mindful of their sensory experiences within their environments and empower them to take actionable steps towards creating spaces that nourish all senses, thus enhancing their wellbeing and happiness. The emphasis is on thoughtful, sensory-focused design as a path to improved quality of life.

**TRANSFORM YOUR SPACE
TRANSFORM YOUR LIFE**

These detailed worksheets aim to guide readers through a deep exploration of how the materials in their environment influence their wellbeing and happiness. This chapter emphasises the emotional, psychological, and physical impacts of various materials used in spaces and encourages readers to make conscious choices that align with their desires for a wellbeing-enhanced environment.

Chapter 5 Worksheets: The Power of Materiality

Worksheet 5.1: Material Mood Board

Objective:
To enable readers to visually compile and reflect on materials that evoke specific feelings or states of wellbeing, facilitating a deeper understanding of materiality's impact on their environment.

**TRANSFORM YOUR SPACE
TRANSFORM YOUR LIFE**

Instructions:

- **Gather Inspiration:** Collect images, samples, or descriptions of materials that you are drawn to. Consider textures, colours, and the overall feel of each material.

- **Create Your Mood Board:** Arrange your collected materials on a board or digital platform. Group them by the feelings they evoke or their intended use in your space.

- **Reflect on Choices:** For each group of materials, note down what feelings they evoke and why you might be drawn to them. Consider how they can enhance your wellbeing.

TRANSFORM YOUR SPACE
TRANSFORM YOUR LIFE

Worksheet:

- **Material Collection**:

- Images/Samples/Descriptions:

**TRANSFORM YOUR SPACE
TRANSFORM YOUR LIFE**

- **Mood Board Sections**:
  - Section 1 (e.g., Warmth, Comfort):
  - Materials:
  - Feelings Evoked:

- (Continue with other sections as needed)

TRANSFORM YOUR SPACE
TRANSFORM YOUR LIFE

- **Reflection**:
  - Material 1:
  - Why I'm Drawn to It:
  - Potential Use:

**TRANSFORM YOUR SPACE
TRANSFORM YOUR LIFE**

Worksheet 5.2: Material Experimentation

Objective: Encourages readers to experiment with different materials in their environment, observing their effects on wellbeing and refining their preferences for future design decisions.

Instructions:

- **Select Materials for Experimentation**: Choose 2-3 materials from your mood board that you are particularly interested in incorporating or experimenting with in your space.

- **Plan Small Changes**: For each selected material, devise a small, manageable change you can make in your environment. This could be adding a textured throw pillow, changing a curtain, or incorporating a wooden piece of decor.

- **Implement and Observe**: Over the course of a month, introduce these changes into your environment. Pay close attention to how each material change affects your mood, productivity, and overall sense of wellbeing.

- **Evaluate and Decide**: At the end of the observation period, evaluate the impact of each material. Decide which changes you'd like to keep, adjust, or remove based on your experiences.

TRANSFORM YOUR SPACE
TRANSFORM YOUR LIFE

Worksheet:

- **Material 1**:
- **Change Implemented**:
- **Observation Period**:
- **Effects Noted**:
- **Decision** (Keep/Adjust/Remove):

- **Material 2**:
- (Repeat the above steps)

**TRANSFORM YOUR SPACE
TRANSFORM YOUR LIFE**

(Continue as needed)

These worksheets are crafted to empower readers to engage thoughtfully with the materials that make up their surroundings, encouraging intentional choices that promote a sense of wellbeing and happiness through the tactile and visual qualities of their environment.

**TRANSFORM YOUR SPACE
TRANSFORM YOUR LIFE**

These worksheets are designed to help readers analyse and redefine the use of different spaces within their environments to maximise wellbeing and happiness. This chapter encourages a thoughtful consideration of how each space serves the individual's needs and how these spaces can be optimised for mental, emotional, and physical health.

Chapter 6 Worksheets: Understanding the Functions of Spaces

Worksheet 6.1: Space Function Analysis

Objective:
To assist readers in evaluating the current function of key spaces in their environment and identifying opportunities for enhancement to better serve their wellbeing.

TRANSFORM YOUR SPACE
TRANSFORM YOUR LIFE

Instructions:

- **List Key Spaces**: Write down the main spaces in your home or work environment (e.g., kitchen, bedroom, living room, office).

- **Current Function Assessment**: For each space listed, describe its current primary function and how it is typically used.

- **Wellbeing Impact Evaluation**: Reflect on how each space currently impacts your wellbeing. Note any positive or negative feelings associated with each space.

- **Ideal Function Definition**: For each space, redefine its ideal function or how it could be modified to better support your wellbeing.

**TRANSFORM YOUR SPACE
TRANSFORM YOUR LIFE**

Worksheet:

- **Space 1 (e.g., Bedroom):**

- **Current Function:**

- **Wellbeing Impact:**

- **Ideal Function:**

TRANSFORM YOUR SPACE
TRANSFORM YOUR LIFE

- (Repeat for each key space)

**TRANSFORM YOUR SPACE
TRANSFORM YOUR LIFE**

Worksheet 6.2: Space Redesign Plan

Objective: To encourage readers to conceptualise a redesign of a chosen space based on the ideal function identified in Worksheet 6.1, with the goal of enhancing wellbeing.

Instructions:

- **Select a Space**: Choose one space from Worksheet 6.1 where changes could have the most significant impact on your wellbeing.

- **Redesign Goals**: Outline specific goals for the redesign, focusing on how the space can better fulfill its ideal function.

- **Design Elements to Introduce/Modify**: List changes to the layout, furniture, colour scheme, lighting, or other elements that could help achieve the redesign goals.

- **Implementation Steps**: Detail the steps needed to accomplish the redesign, including any necessary purchases, rearrangements, or decluttering.

- **Timeline and Budget**: Set a realistic timeline and budget for the redesign project.

**TRANSFORM YOUR SPACE
TRANSFORM YOUR LIFE**

Worksheet:

- **Chosen Space:**
- **Redesign Goals:**
    - **Design Elements:**
    - Layout:
    - Furniture:
    - Colour Scheme:
    - Lighting:
    - Others:
    - **Implementation Steps:**
    - Step 1:
    - Step 2:

TRANSFORM YOUR SPACE
TRANSFORM YOUR LIFE

- (Continue as needed)

- **Timeline**:
- **Budget**:

These worksheets guide readers through a methodical approach to rethinking the use and design of their spaces. By focusing on the function of each space and its impact on wellbeing, readers can make informed decisions on redesigns and adjustments that foster a supportive and fulfilling environment.

**TRANSFORM YOUR SPACE
TRANSFORM YOUR LIFE**

These worksheets are crafted to guide readers through recognising and adapting the primal needs met by our living environments to the demands and stresses of modern life. The chapter draws parallels between ancient habitats and contemporary spaces, focusing on how understanding our primal needs can inform better design choices that promote wellbeing and happiness.

Chapter 7 Worksheets: Modern Day Cavemen

Worksheet 7.1: Primal Needs Assessment

Objective:
To help readers identify how their current living or working environments meet their primal needs for safety, comfort, and community, and where there might be gaps.

**TRANSFORM YOUR SPACE
TRANSFORM YOUR LIFE**

Instructions:

- **List Primal Needs**: Reflect on the primal needs that any living space should meet, such as safety, comfort, privacy, social interaction, and connection with nature.

- **Current Environment Assessment**: For each primal need listed, assess how well your current living or working environment meets this need. Use a scale of 1-10, where 1 is not met at all, and 10 is fully met.

- **Identify Gaps**: Highlight any needs that score below 5, indicating areas for improvement in your environment.

TRANSFORM YOUR SPACE
TRANSFORM YOUR LIFE

Worksheet:

- **Primal Need**: Safety
- **Assessment Score**:
- **Notes/Comments**:

- **Primal Need**: Comfort
- **Assessment Score**:
- **Notes/Comments**:

**TRANSFORM YOUR SPACE
TRANSFORM YOUR LIFE**

- (Continue for each primal need)

TRANSFORM YOUR SPACE
TRANSFORM YOUR LIFE

Worksheet 7.2: Enhancing Primal Comforts

Objective: Encourages readers to develop strategies for enhancing their environment to better meet primal needs, inspired by the concept of modern-day cavemen.

Instructions:

- **Select a Need to Address**: Choose one primal need from Worksheet 7.1 that you would like to focus on improving in your environment.

- **Brainstorm Enhancements**: For the selected need, brainstorm specific enhancements or changes to your space that could better fulfill this need. Consider incorporating elements that mimic natural habitats or foster a sense of security and belonging.

- **Plan of Action**: Develop a concrete plan of action for implementing these enhancements. Include any necessary purchases, rearrangements, or modifications to your space.

- **Expected Outcome**: Describe how you anticipate these changes will improve your wellbeing and happiness in your environment.

TRANSFORM YOUR SPACE
TRANSFORM YOUR LIFE

Worksheet:

- **Selected Primal Need**:
    - **Enhancements**:
        - **Element 1**:
        - **Action Steps**:

        - **Element 2**:
        - **Action Steps**:

    - (Add more elements as needed)
    - **Plan of Action**:
    - Step 1:

    - Step 2:

**TRANSFORM YOUR SPACE
TRANSFORM YOUR LIFE**

- (Continue as needed)

- **Expected Outcome:**

These worksheets aim to bridge the gap between our ancient instincts and the realities of modern living. By focusing on primal needs and how well they are met in our current environments, readers are encouraged to make mindful adjustments that enhance their overall sense of wellbeing and fulfillment, aligning modern spaces with our deep-rooted needs.

**TRANSFORM YOUR SPACE
TRANSFORM YOUR LIFE**

These worksheets focus on understanding and enhancing the social dynamics within our living and working environments. This chapter emphasises the importance of community and social connections in our spaces, drawing on the concept that, like our ancestors who lived in tribes, modern humans also thrive in supportive social settings.

Chapter 8 Worksheets:

Tribes

Worksheet 8.1: Social Space Audit

Objective:
To help readers assess the social dynamics of their environments and identify opportunities to foster a sense of community and belonging.

TRANSFORM YOUR SPACE
TRANSFORM YOUR LIFE

Instructions:

- **Map Your Key Environments**: List the primary spaces where you spend your time (e.g., home, office, community center).

- **Current Social Dynamics**: For each space, describe the current social interactions and sense of community. Consider frequency, quality, and the nature of these interactions.

- **Community Feelings**: Rate how connected and supported you feel in each environment on a scale of 1-10, where 1 is not at all, and 10 is fully supported.

- **Opportunities for Enhancement**: Identify opportunities within each space to improve social connections and foster a stronger sense of community.

**TRANSFORM YOUR SPACE
TRANSFORM YOUR LIFE**

Worksheet:

- **Space**: Home
- **Current Social Dynamics**:

- **Community Feelings Score**:

- **Enhancement Opportunities**:

**TRANSFORM YOUR SPACE
TRANSFORM YOUR LIFE**

- (Repeat for other key environments)

**TRANSFORM YOUR SPACE
TRANSFORM YOUR LIFE**

Worksheet 8.2: Designing for Community

Objective: Encourages readers to create a plan for redesigning a selected space to better support social interactions and build a sense of community.

Instructions:

- **Choose a Space for Enhancement**: From the spaces listed in Worksheet 8.1, select one where enhancing social connections could have the most significant impact.

- **Community Design Goals**: Define specific goals for how the space can be redesigned to foster community (e.g., more open gathering areas, communal dining spaces).

- **Design Elements and Strategies**: List changes to the layout, furniture, or other design elements that could help achieve your community design goals.

- **Implementation Plan and Timeline**: Detail the steps necessary to transform the space, including any required resources or assistance. Set a timeline for these changes.

**TRANSFORM YOUR SPACE
TRANSFORM YOUR LIFE**

Worksheet:

- **Selected Space:**
- **Community Design Goals:**
    - **Design Elements and Strategies:**
    - Layout Changes:
    - Furniture Additions/Modifications:

    - Other Design Strategies:

**TRANSFORM YOUR SPACE
TRANSFORM YOUR LIFE**

- **Implementation Plan**:

- Step 1:

- Step 2:

- Step 3:

**TRANSFORM YOUR SPACE
TRANSFORM YOUR LIFE**

- (Continue as needed)

- **Timeline**:

These worksheets are designed to enhance the reader's awareness of the social aspects of their environments. By evaluating and planning improvements to foster better social interactions and a sense of community, readers can create spaces that not only meet their physical and aesthetic needs but also their social and emotional ones, reflecting the essential human need for connection and belonging.

TRANSFORM YOUR SPACE
TRANSFORM YOUR LIFE

These worksheets are geared towards optimising the three critical areas of the home that significantly impact our daily wellbeing: the dining area, kitchen, and sleeping environment. This chapter underscores the unique role each area plays in nurturing our health, happiness, and social connections, emphasising thoughtful design and usage.

Chapter 9 Worksheets: DKZzzz (Dining/Kitchen/Sleep)

Worksheet 9.1: DKZzz Analysis

Objective:
To assist readers in evaluating how their dining area, kitchen, and sleeping environment currently serve their wellbeing and identifying areas for improvement.

**TRANSFORM YOUR SPACE
TRANSFORM YOUR LIFE**

Instructions:

- **Assess Each Area:** Reflect on your dining area, kitchen and sleeping environment. Consider aspects like comfort, functionality, aesthetics, and their contribution to your wellbeing.

- **Wellbeing Impact Evaluation**: For each area, assess how it currently impacts your physical, emotional, and social wellbeing. Use a scale of 1-10, where 1 is negative impact and 10 is highly positive impact.

- **Identify Improvement Opportunities**: Note down specific aspects of each area that could be improved to better support your wellbeing.

**TRANSFORM YOUR SPACE
TRANSFORM YOUR LIFE**

Worksheet:

- **Area**: Dining
- **Current Assessment**:

- **Wellbeing Impact Score**:

- **Improvement Opportunities**:

TRANSFORM YOUR SPACE
TRANSFORM YOUR LIFE

- **Area**: Kitchen
- **Current Assessment**:

- **Wellbeing Impact Score**:

- **Improvement Opportunities**:

TRANSFORM YOUR SPACE
TRANSFORM YOUR LIFE

- **Area**: Sleep
- **Current Assessment**:

- **Wellbeing Impact Score**:

- **Improvement Opportunities**:

**TRANSFORM YOUR SPACE
TRANSFORM YOUR LIFE**

Worksheet 9.2: Wellbeing Enhancement Plan

Objective:

Encourages readers to devise a practical plan for enhancing their dining, kitchen, and sleeping areas based on the analysis from Worksheet 9.1, with the aim of improving overall wellbeing.

Instructions:

- **Select Priorities**: Based on Worksheet 9.1, choose one improvement opportunity for each area (dining, kitchen, sleep) to focus on.

- **Plan Enhancements**: For the selected improvement opportunities, detail the ehancements or changes you plan to make. Consider layout adjustments, new habits, additions or removals of furniture or items, lighting changes, etc.

- **Action Steps**: Break down each enhancement into actionable steps, including any needed resources, purchases, or help from others.

- **Set Goals and Timeline**: Define what success looks like for each enhancement and set a realistic timeline for implementing these changes.

**TRANSFORM YOUR SPACE
TRANSFORM YOUR LIFE**

Worksheet:

- **Improvement Priority for Dining:**

- **Planned Enhancements:**

- **Action Steps:**

- **Success Goals:**
- **Timeline:**

**TRANSFORM YOUR SPACE
TRANSFORM YOUR LIFE**

- **Improvement Priority for Kitchen:**

- (Repeat the above steps)

**TRANSFORM YOUR SPACE
TRANSFORM YOUR LIFE**

- **Improvement Priority for Sleep:**

- (Repeat the above steps)

These worksheets are crafted to guide readers through a mindful examination of their dining, kitchen, and sleep environments, encouraging strategic enhancements that promote physical, emotional, and social wellbeing. By focusing on these essential home areas, readers can create a more nurturing and supportive living space conducive to their overall happiness and health.

**TRANSFORM YOUR SPACE
TRANSFORM YOUR LIFE**

These worksheets are designed to encapsulate the essence of the book's teachings and guide readers in crafting a forward-looking plan. This chapter focuses on integrating all the insights and strategies from previous chapters to create a cohesive action plan that enhances wellbeing and happiness through thoughtful architecture and design in their living and working environments.

Chapter 10 Worksheets: How to WHAD Ahead?

Worksheet 10.1: WHAD Reflection

Objective:
To facilitate a comprehensive reflection on the key insights and lessons learned from each chapter, helping readers to conceptualise how they can apply these learnings to their environments moving forward.

**TRANSFORM YOUR SPACE
TRANSFORM YOUR LIFE**

Instructions:

- **Chapter Reflections**: For each chapter (1-9), write a brief reflection on the most impactful insight or lesson you took away and how it relates to your personal or work environment.

- **Integration Ideas**: Based on your reflections, list ideas on how you can integrate these insights into your living or working spaces to enhance wellbeing and happiness.

**TRANSFORM YOUR SPACE
TRANSFORM YOUR LIFE**

Worksheet:

- **Chapter 1 (SBB: Small but Big):**
- **Reflection:**

- **Integration Idea:**

**TRANSFORM YOUR SPACE
TRANSFORM YOUR LIFE**

- **Chapter 2 (The EUREKA of WHAD):**
- **Reflection:**

- **Integration Idea:**

-

**TRANSFORM YOUR SPACE
TRANSFORM YOUR LIFE**

- (Continue for each chapter)

**TRANSFORM YOUR SPACE
TRANSFORM YOUR LIFE**

- (Continue for each chapter)

**TRANSFORM YOUR SPACE
TRANSFORM YOUR LIFE**

- (Continue for each chapter)

**TRANSFORM YOUR SPACE
TRANSFORM YOUR LIFE**

- (Continue for each chapter)

**TRANSFORM YOUR SPACE
TRANSFORM YOUR LIFE**

Worksheet 10.2: WHAD Action Plan

Objective: To empower readers to create a detailed, actionable plan for implementing the changes and enhancements identified in their reflections, ensuring a holistic approach to utilising architecture and design for wellbeing.

Instructions:

- **Prioritise Actions**: From the integration ideas listed in Worksheet 10.1, prioritise the actions based on their potential impact on your wellbeing and feasibility.

- **Detailed Action Steps**: For each priority action, outline specific steps needed to implement this change, including resources, timeframe, and any potential challenges.

- **Set Milestones**: Establish milestones for tracking progress on each action, allowing for adjustments as needed.

- **Visualise Success**: For each action, visualise and describe the expected outcome and its impact on your wellbeing and happiness.

TRANSFORM YOUR SPACE
TRANSFORM YOUR LIFE

Worksheet:

- **Priority Action 1:**
- **Action Steps:**

- **Milestones:**

- **Visualised Success:**

TRANSFORM YOUR SPACE
TRANSFORM YOUR LIFE

- **Priority Action 2:**

- **Action Steps:**

- **Milestones:**

- **Visualised Success:**

**TRANSFORM YOUR SPACE
TRANSFORM YOUR LIFE**

- **Priority Action 3:**

- **Action Steps:**

- **Milestones:**

- **Visualised Success:**

TRANSFORM YOUR SPACE
TRANSFORM YOUR LIFE

- **Priority Action 4:**

- **Action Steps:**

- **Milestones:**

- **Visualised Success:**

TRANSFORM YOUR SPACE
TRANSFORM YOUR LIFE

- **Priority Action 5:**
- **Action Steps:**

- **Milestones:**

- **Visualised Success:**

**TRANSFORM YOUR SPACE
TRANSFORM YOUR LIFE**

- **All other insights**

**TRANSFORM YOUR SPACE
TRANSFORM YOUR LIFE**

CELEBRATE
how far you have come

TRANSFORM YOUR SPACE
TRANSFORM YOUR LIFE

YOUR NOTES

**TRANSFORM YOUR SPACE
TRANSFORM YOUR LIFE**

YOUR NOTES

**TRANSFORM YOUR SPACE
TRANSFORM YOUR LIFE**

YOUR NOTES

**TRANSFORM YOUR SPACE
TRANSFORM YOUR LIFE**

CONGRATULATIONS!

These worksheets are crafted to ensure that the teachings of

"Wellbeing + Happiness thru' Architecture + Design"

are not just theoretical but are actively applied by the readers in their own spaces.

By reflecting on each chapter's lessons and planning actionable steps, readers are equipped to make informed decisions and changes that foster environments conducive to wellbeing and happiness, embodying the WHAD philosophy in their daily lives.

**TRANSFORM YOUR SPACE
TRANSFORM YOUR LIFE**

www.ingramcontent.com/pod-product-compliance
Lightning Source LLC
Chambersburg PA
CBHW071219070526
44584CB00019B/3074